The Constructive
of Marriage

The Constructive of Marriage

Dr. Ramses Charles

Doctor of Philosophy in Christian Counseling
Ph.D.

authorHOUSE®

AuthorHouse™ LLC
1663 Liberty Drive
Bloomington, IN 47403
www.authorhouse.com
Phone: 1-800-839-8640

Published by AuthorHouse   11/21/2013

ISBN: 978-1-4918-3837-2 (sc)
ISBN: 978-1-4918-3836-5 (hc)
ISBN: 978-1-4918-3835-8 (e)

Library of Congress Control Number: 2013921582

I dedicate this book to my family, the greatest help in the world. Each filled with personality and dons and a great smile.

Finally, my admirable wife, *Marie A. Charles,* and my children, *Steve R. Charles, McRolph Charles* and *Christopher Charles.* All of them always remain close to me.

Contents

Acknowledgements

The human being life is not a good characteristic way to get better like everyone knew. Yet the obstacles to the man well-being. Personal economic, social, and geopolitical are formidable. But the other term let's know you could be changed the life that depends on what you want.

The best route of the life means to follow the rules we would have gotten something in the different way and then follow the best person like God.

The Constructive of Marriage

Introduction:

Since the beginning of human life in the earth, Marriage has been the central feature of all human societies, an institution composed of a culturally accepted union of a man and a woman in a husband-wife relationship as well as roles that recognize an order of sexual behavior and legalize the function of parenthood.

Marriage was instituted by God when he declared, "It is not good that man should be alone. I will make him a helper comparable to him." (Gen. 2:8). So God fashioned a woman and brought her to the man. Upon seeing the woman, Adam exclaimed, "This is now bone of my bones and flesh of my flesh; she shall be called woman because she was taken out of man." (Gen. 2:23).

"This passage also emphasizes the truth that a man shall leave his father and mother and be joined to his wife, and they shall become one flesh." (Gen. 2:24). This suggests that God's ideal is for a man to be the husband of one woman and for the marriage to be permanent.

In the time of marital instability, sociologists and marriage counselors have bought more exact, value laden definitions of the categories within marriage. Thus Lederer and Jackson (1968) designated for: The stable satisfactory, the stable unsatisfactory marriages. Cuber and Harroff (1977), on the other hand, have divided marriages into the total, the vital, the passive-con-genial, the conflict-habituated, and the devitalized. Their study forced them to the extremely depressing conclusion that few good marital relationships in which the communication is more satisfying than that in marriage.

The reasons why people marry vary widely and cover a spectrum in a stable, rational society, marriage is valued for its ordering of relationships. Through its property is allocated and passed on to heirs. By its intimate companionship between a man and woman is defined, progeny are provided for and protected, and families are organized.

Historically, marriage has also regulated sexual intercourse, a regulation once again vigorously challenged by many, and certainly not for the first time. God's desire for his people was for them to marry within the body of believers. The Mosaic law clearly stated that, "an Israelite was never to marry a foreigner. The Israelite would be constantly tempted to embrace the spouse's God as well." (Ex. 34:10)(17), (Deut. 7:3-4). Likewise, the apostle Paul commanded the members of the church at Corinth, "Do not be unequally yoked together with unbelievers." (2 Cor. 6:14).

Jesus' first miracle occurred in Cana in Galilee when he and his disciples were attending a wedding (John 2:1-11). Our lord gave his blessing and sanction to the institution of marriage on another occasion. When Jesus was asked about marriage and divorce, he gusted two passages from Genesis. Have you not read that he who made them at the beginning made them male and female; and said, "For this reason a man shall leave his father and mother and be joined to his wife, and the two shall become one flesh?" So then, they are no longer two but one flesh.

Therefore what God has joined together, let not man separate (Gen. 1:27, 2:24; Mat. 19:4-6). He taught that marriage was the joining together of two people so they can become one flesh. Not only did God acknowledge the marriage, he also joined the couple.

The church at Corinth struggled over a member of issues, including the proper view of marriage. In response to their questions, Paul gave an answer about marriage. From his answer, it seemed that three faulty ideas about marriage were prominent among some believers in the church. The first was that marriage was absolutely necessary in order to be a Christian; another was that celibacy was superior to marriage; the third was that when a person became a Christian, all existing relationships such as marriage were dissolved.

When chapter seven of 1 Corinthians is read with that as a background, the following teaching emerges. Paul stated that celibacy is an acceptable lifestyle for a Christian; not all people need to marry. So Paul declared that he himself prepared not to marry, however, the single life can be lived for God's glory only if it has been given the gift of singlehood.

If one does not have that gift, he should; and Paul expected most people to marry. Next Paul spoke to the problem faced by a Christian believer whose spouse does not believe. He reasoned that if the unbelieving partner is willing to live with the Christian, then the Christian should not dissolve the marriage. Remaining with the unbelieving partner could result in his or her salvation (1 Cor. 7:14).

In his letter to the Ephesians, Paul showed how a marriage relationship can best function. First, he said, "Wives, submit to your husbands, as to the Lord" (Eph. 5:22).

The model for the wife's submission is in the church, which is subject to Christ (Eph. 5:24). Second, husbands are to love their wives. The role that the husband plays is outlined by Jesus Christ, who loved his bride, the church, so much that he died for her (Eph. 5:25).

Chapter 1

What is the Constructive of Marriage?

Marriage creates the basic social unit of family, community and society. The meaning of marriage in Biblical literature ascribes to marriage a two-fold purpose, Procreation (Gen. 1:28) and Companionship (Gen. 2:18). To these two purposes the Talmud adds a third, the fulfillment of oneself as a person.

He who has no wife is not a proper man; he lives without joy, blessing, goodness, protection and peace. Jewish tradition regards marriage as the idea of human state. While celibacy was advocated by the essences, the mainstream of Jewish thought looks upon it with disfavor since it does not permit the individual to procreate and thereby fulfill one's basic obligation to society.

Although the Talmud refers to the sexual urge as yeter ha-ra (lit., the evil inclination), it is basically not regarded as evil. Because the sex drive is such a powerful force in human life, it must be contained within the bounds of marriage and controlled by limitations on permissibility even within that framework. When thus moderated, it is a powerful motivating force which serves good end.

Where it is not for the yeter ha-ra, no man would build a house, marry a woman or have children. While polygamy was permissible during the Biblical period and until the Takama a decree for the betterment of society not based upon traditional Jewish law of Robenu Gershom around the year 1,000 C.E., it was practiced primarily by the upper classes.

Even in Biblical times the norm was that a man had only one wife. This is corroborated by the prophets' use of marriage as a metaphor for the relationship between God and Israel, and by the metaphorical interpretation of the Song of Songs. While polygamy was still possible in Talmudic times, it was almost unknown. Marriage was prohibited among close relatives. The Biblical laurs of incest were supplemented and expanded in the Talmud and became the basic of incest laws throughout Western civilization.

During the Biblical period, endogamous marriages were encouraged while exogamous marriages were opposed in order to protect the community from idolatry and to preserve Jewish identity.

Although marriage is not a sacrament in the Christian sense of the word and can be dissolved by divorce (Deut. 24:1-4), it is considered a sacred relationship. The Hebrew word for marriage is Kiddusbin (lit., sanctification). In marriage, the wife is consecrated or set apart to her husband. While the legal obligations of husband and wife and their respective families were traditionally defined in the Ketubal (marriage document), the couple also had the moral obligations of love, honor and respect for each other.

In traditional marriage, ceremony has two parts: Erusin, the betrothal, and Nissu'in the marriage proper.

In Talmudic times, the two ceremonies could be separated married erusin, cohabitation could not take place until nissu'in. This posed many practical and legal difficulties for the couple as well as for the Jewish community. Consequently in post-Talmudic times, the two ceremonies were combined into one. This has been the accepted practice since the Twelfth Century except in a few oriental communities.

A marriage ceremony may be performed in any location, since sanctity in Jewish tradition resides not in a place but rather in the purpose for which a place is used. It may be held on any day of the week except for the Sabbath or a festival when the signing of a legal document is prohibited in tradition Judaism. While technically this prohibition does not apply in Reform Judaism, the custom of not holding a wedding on the Sabbath or a festival is so rooted in tradition that it is almost uniformly adhered to.

The marriage enrichment movement and methodology began in Spain in January 1962 under the leadership of Father Gabriel Calvo, and in the U.S. this program became known as marriage encounter. David and Vera Mace began marriage enrichment with Quaker couples in October 1962 and 1973. They had organized the association of couples for marriage enrichment (ACME); within a decade several thousand lay and professional couples in all fifty states held membership in ACME.

In the US, the movement has been closely associated with religious faith groups, and some fifteen national programs are directly connected to an established religious organization.

Many programs are localized but some of the more prominent national programs are: Marriage Encounter (ME), Marriage Communication Labs (MCL), Relationship Enhancement Programs (RE), Couples Communicational Programs (CCP), and Training in Marriage Enrichment (TIME), listening and loving Practical Application of Intimate Relationship Skills (PAIRS) and the Association of Couples for Marriage Enrichment (ACME).

In 1975, the Council of Affiliated Marriage Enrichment Organizations (CAMEO) was formed with a major concern to establish standards for leadership training, but a system of national certification of leaders and accreditation of training centers is yet to be developed. The states aim is to make good marriage better and implicitly, the goal is to foster personal growth and mutual fulfillment in enough marriage that the public image of marriage as a fulfillment relationship will be enhanced. A growth oriented, potential oriented perspective of the individual and a dynamic view of the martial system is employed to promote an intentional companionship model of marriage in the varied programs.

Experimental, relational inductive methods of education are employed to enhance communicational skill and alter behavior or individual with the primary objective of enriching the marital relationship. But prevention of marital dysfunction is also perceived to be as important as intervention or correction. Methodologically, the programs focus on the couple relationship through self-disclosure of feelings and thoughts concentrate on the present tense and the positive strengths of the mates, teach communicational skill, accept conflict positively and resolve it creatively, seek behavioral and attitudinal change advocate a companionship model of marriage and enable the renegotiating of commitments and the reforming of contracts.

There is some indication that the movement has contributed significantly to the stabilizing of marriage and that the programs have enhanced marital relationship in middle class Americans. Sufficient research data has not been collected to verify either the types of individuals served or to identify the specific relationship changes that have been produced or the stability of the changes over a period of the time. Also, some questions about the movement have been raised from both clinical and theological perspective.

Among the clinical concerns are: the lack of selectivity or screening of the participant the seeming little appreciation of the power of resistance and anticipatory grief in the promulgation of instant intimacy, the assumption that enhancement of a relationship follows better communication, the arrested focus on intimacy between equal self-fulfilled individuals, and the lack of structured after care and or sufficient attention to the reentry of participants following their weekend retreat.

Marriage encounter, however, has developed a follow up structure involving a monthly couples group. Theological concerns that have been related to the movement are implicit humanism and their implicit promotion of a new church mentality. Theologically along with enticing persons to make their marriage more perfect by mastering skills of sharing feelings, the movement might also give greater acknowledgement to the ambiguity, the frailty, and the incompleteness of human existence.

Otherwise it may be in danger of implicitly encouraging persons to be committed to a little more than instant gratification of immediate impulsive feelings within the closed system of the couple. But marriage is considered a major role in Christian marriage, even though the institution of marriage is not intrinsically Christian, and its presence throughout time and space has been recognized quite apart from any theological considerations. In Christian doctrine, marriage fulfills God's plan of creation, for we were created in the marriage in the image of God, and blessed as male and female (Gen. 1:27).

Moreover the doctrine of Christian marriage is so integrally built into existence that it provides a paradigm for God's relation to humanity. In a cosmic analogy, God is to us as a loving husband is to his wife (Jer. 31:32; Isa. 54:5) and this ratio cination is echoed where Christ is pictured as the bride-groom in the synoptic gospels as well as in the writings of Paul (2 Cor. 11:2).

From these and similar passages, Christians may deduce that the mystical wedding of God-in-Christ to the church is an archetype for human marriage. Throughout the Bible, marriage is considered a covenant (Serith) whose very nature is fidelity. The covenant is not only between husband and wife, but also between that couple and God. Unlike a legal contract whose agreement may be broken when conditions change, this covenant is binding for better, for worse, for richer, for poorer, in sickness and in health. It partakes of the age-old covenantal characteristic; that is, it is a freely made promise that will involve an obligatory task, and it is negotiated for permanence. It includes witnesses and social family support; it can be renewed and it enjoys the blessing of God whose promise seals it.

The once-heated debate between Protestant and Roman Catholic Christians over whether marriage is a sacrament has been subsiding. It stemmed from a tridentate dogma, which had been based on a translation of mysterion (Eph. 5:32) as sacramentum. This complex doctrine from Paul's metaphysical concept of psychophysical bonds was seen at the council of Trent as a mystical union. As regulated by the Roman Catholic Church. Marriage is conferred on one another by a baptized woman and a baptized man marrying in the presence of witnesses. With Christian faith present, this sacrament of marriage mediates a means of divine grace.

The Concept of Social Relationship

The term "social relationship" will be used to designate the situation where two or more persons are engaged in conduct wherein each takes account of the behavior of the other in a meaningful way and is therefore oriented in these terms. The social relationship thus consists entirely of the probability that individuals will behave in some meaningfully determinable way.

It is completely irrelevant why such a probability exists, but where it does there can be found a social relationship.

1) A defining criterion therefore demands at least a minimum of natural orientation of the conduct of each to that of the other. Its content may be most varied: conflict, hostility, sexual attraction, friendship, loyalty or severance of an agreement, economic, erotic, or any other form of competition, a sharing of occupations or membership in the some class or nation. In the later cases, these memberships may not constitute social conduct,

as will be discussed later. Furthermore, the definition does not inform as to the degree of solidarity, or its opposite, prevailing among those engaged in this conduct.

2) It is always a case if used in this context of the meaning imputed to those individuals involved in a given concrete situation, either on the average or in theoretically constructed pure type but it is never a case of normatively correct or metaphorically true meaning. The social relationship consist even in the case of such social organizations as a state, church association or marriage in the fact that there has existed, exists, or will exist a probable conduct in some definition way appropriate to this meaning. It is necessary to emphasize this in order to avoid the rectification of these concepts, their degeneration into empty conceptualization. Thus a state loses is sociological significance, as soon as it is probable that it ceases to manifest any kind of meaningfully oriented social behavior. Such probability may be very high or it may be insignificant, but in any case it is only in the sense and degree in which it does exist or can be estimated to exist that the corresponding relationship exists. Otherwise no other meaning can be given to the phrase that a given state exists or has ceased to exist.

3) All parties who are mutually oriented in a given social relationship do not necessarily manifest the same subjective meaning about it, there need not be any reciprocity. Friendships,

love, loyalty, contractual trust and nationalism, on the other side, may well be faced with an entirely different attitude on the other. To the parties involved, their conduct merely shows various forms and meanings, and the social relationship is simply asymmetrical. Nevertheless, they may be mutually oriented in so far as one party presumes a particular attitude toward himself on the part of the other and orient his own conduct accordingly.

Regardless of whether or not he is mistaken in his expectations, this can and usually will result in a certain course of conduct and will have consequence for the form of the relationship exists only if in their expectations of this relationship it means the same to all parties involved. For example, the actual attitude of a child to its father may be at least approximately that which the father on the whole, has to expect. A social relationship in which the attitudes are completely and fully oriented toward each other is really a marginal case. According to our terminology, the absence of reciprocity will exclude the existence of a social relationship only if such mutual orientation is really lacking in the behavior of the parties. Here and elsewhere, all sorts of transitional cases are the rule rather than the exception.

4) A social relationship can be of a transitory nature or of varying degrees of permanence. That is, it can be of such a kind that there is a probability of the repeated recurrence of the

behavior which corresponds to its subjective meaning and is therefore expected because it is in consequence of such meaning.

But in order to avoid giving false impressions, it bears repetition to remember that it is only the existence of the probability that corresponding to a given subjective meaning complex, a certain type of behavior will take place which constitutes the existence of the social relationship. Thus, that friendship or state exists or has existed means only this: that in the judgment of us, the probability that given certain kinds of known subjective attitude of certain individuals, there will result, on the average, a certain specific type of conduct and nothing else (compare above with No. 2). The unavoidable alternative from the legal point of view: whether or not a rule of law is endowed with legal validity and a legal relationship therefore can be assumed to exist, such a simple alternative is not relevant to sociological problems.

5) The subjective meaning of a social relationship may change for example, a political relationship or marriage relationship may change, from one based on solidarity into one based on conflict. But then it is simply a question of terminological convenience and of the degree of continuity of the change, whether it is said that a new relationship has come into existence or that the old one continues but has acquired new meaning. The meaning too can waver between constancy and permanency.

The meaningful content which remains relatively constant in a social relationship is capable of being expressed in axioms to which the parties involved can be expected to adhere at least approximately by their partners. This is the most likely to be the case, the more rational the conduct is in relation to give values or goals. There is far less possibility of rational formulation of subjective meaning in the case of an erotic attraction or a relation based on personal loyalty or any other emotional type than there is, for example, in the case of a business contract.

The meaning of a social relationship can be agreed to by mutual consent. This means that those who participate make promises concerning theirs or any other way. Each participant expects then that normally, and insofar as he behaves rationally, the other participant will orient this behavior in accordance with the meaning of the argument as the first participant understands it. His own behavior is thus partly goal-oriented and he expects to adhere more or less loyalty to it, but it is also partly value related, that is, it is his duty to adhere to the argument in the sense as he understands it.

Marriage Ethics

Chronological marriage ethics in the New Testament times continued many of these customs, but redefined the relationship in terms of Christ and the Church marriage had now become a symbol of the kingdom of God. We have little existent evidence of any nuptial right, except that it gradually involved evolved into an adaptation of contemporary customs that featured the presence of a Bishop and a Eucharist.

Mutuality in the Lord was the key element (Eph. 5:21); tenderness to another was enjoined (1 Peter 3:7); and the unitive relationship was emphasized (Mark 10:8). Nowhere in the New Testament is sexual intercourse understood to be exclusively for the procreation of children; the one-flesh bond of marriage is normative. By this time polygamy had been super seded by monogamy; a higher place was accorded to women (Gal 3:28); and both husband and wife are considered joint heirs of the grace of life. The commitment to fidelity in the relationship and the expectation of its permanence are stressed: What God has joined together let not man put as under (Mark 10:9).

The most important concept of marriage has been growing in recent years. The purpose of marriage has been in henosis, that one-flesh relationship of cohumanite with all other ends as secondary. Just as Vatican II avoided ranking mutuality and procreation as respectively primary and secondary ends, so a reawakened theology has been moving to view Christian marriage more in interpersonal than in functional term. This has enabled couples to see their marriage as a process of growing relationship, their failures as potentially forgivable, and their life together as pilgrimage.

In contemporary issue of marriage, it is impermanence and instability that concern most observers of the marital scene today. The ratio of one divorce decree to every two marriage licenses is but one indication. To that must be added the annulments the emotional divorces of those who remain together in the same house but without intimate relationship, and those whose recurrent strife makes a mockery of their matrimony.

The ubique-tous breakdown of marriage show up some couples who are individually well adjusted but wed in combinations that are maladjusted some persons who lack marital aptitude, and others who view marriage as a temporary connection.

Thus many divorces may represent unions that had been stable for a time but were incapable of so continuing. Changing roles of women and men around the world have profoundly altered marital expectations. The struggle between a new sexual egalitarianism and an older double standard promotes strife in numerous couples.

Power equalization is counterbalanced by traditionalism (Persons and Bales, 1955) and complicated by resentment and communication failure. The interweaving of habit systems in marital relations traditionally interlocks our customs by cross-influence and continuity (Waller and Hill, 1955). Roles are changing but they change gradually. The conflict issues are difficulty to rank as they change both in year and in area. Yet among the problems that stand out will usually be found control, fear of abandonment, discipline of children, sexual disappointment, spending of money, relations with-in-law, lack of consideration, infidelity, and violence.

Today's major marital differences tend to include fewer of the social distinctions over which past generations fouth; ethnic, religious, class, and cultural issues. The increasing number of mixed marriage across such lines is clear indication of our growing pluralism and toleration. As marriage changes from institution to companionship to system, it moves also to a desacralized secular status and demands a more highly adaptive family system than any we have been in the past.

Researchers, seeking clues for stabilizing marriage, have investigated the congruence of satisfaction between husbands and wives; their assumption being that live interests hold a couple together. But the hypothesis could not be verified by evidence.

Others, with a diametrical assumption, have supposed that complementarity by attracting opposites could keep marriage alive through the mutual fulfilling of needs. But research evidence fails also to substantiate this theory. Similarities and differences between the sexes are important in the ways they are perceived by the persons. Larger differences emerge from the changes that mates experience through development and their interactive relationships in those passages. A gradual decline in marital satisfaction can be measured in most couples over a period of time. Although there are wide variations in the trend (e.g. lower economic classes exhibit the sharper decline according to Komarovsky) the tendency is marked and disillusionment can result. Determination in marital stability prompts all the helping professions to seek methods of education and enrichment that enable couples to survive their changes in role and development and to persevere through periods of adjustment.

Imaginative and varied programs have been devised from written contracts to behavioral modification in order to arrest the breakdown of marriage, for it is widely recognized that our society is not so vigorous that it can forego the ideals and values that uphold marital permanence and family life.

For the future of marriage, it is to be expected that the divorce rate will level off that equality between the sexes will improve, that sexual fidelity and monogamy will be norm, though with a current pattern of alternative styles in marriage.

The divorce rate is likely to continue at a high figure; for the countervailing social and spiritual forces are not organized to reserve it. Indeed the trend is abetted by the ready availability of divorce, the approbation of friends, and the economic situation that now allows both sexes to achieve financial independence. The proliferation of alternative styles is certain to expand beyond the living-together arrangements, group marriage and serial marriages of today.

With the measurable increase of households among single persons, single parents, child-free marriage, and smaller families, it is predictable that new patterns will also emerge even from these.

Inevitably, though slowly, new sex symmetry is replacing male domination in society. Dual employment of couples, their separate careers, and the liberated political awareness of women contribute to this expectation. Gradually the tension felt among older husbands will subside and a stronger relationship of marital equality will emerge. Though still at a disadvantage in career and status, women are advancing to a place of parity.

Although premarital sexual activity is now institutionalized through much of our culture and a greater quantity of sexual activity is measurable both within and outside marriage most sexual contact remains contained within marriage.

Dissatisfactions with sexual freedom, attested by experienced persons often lead to recommitment to word sexual exclusivity in marriage though clearly not the preference of a significant minority, fidelity does however establish the norm. Despite the spread of alternative marital styles and the notable toleration of these, monogamy will continue to be the standard by which all forms of marital relationship are evaluated. A conventional expectation of wedding fidelity, child rearing, and mutuality will prevail. Even in the face of shorter contracts for marriage will obtain for the majority and remain as a societal standard.

Chapter 2

Interpersonal Issues

Characteristic forms of social conduct like any other form of conduct social conduct may be determined in any one of the following four ways. First it may be classified rationally and oriented toward a goal.

In this instance the classification is based on the expectation that objects in the external situation or other human individual will behave in a certain way, and by the use of such expectations as conditions or means for the successful achievement of the individual's own rationally chosen goals. Such a case will be called goal oriented conduct. Second, conduct maybe classified by the conscious belief in the absolute worth of the conduct. As such, independent of any ulterior motive and measured by some such standard as ethics, esthetics or religion such a case of rational orientation toward an absolute value will be called value related conduct. Third, social conduct may be classified affectually, especially emotionally the result of a special confirmation of feeling and emotions on the part of the individual.

Fourth, social conduct may be classified traditionally, having been accustomed to by long practice. Strictly traditionalist behavior just as the reactive type of imitation discussed above lies altogether on the borderline and sometimes even crosses what can be called meaningful oriented conduct. Frequently it is simply a dull reaction almost oriented conduct to accustomed stimuli that have led behavior repeatedly along a routine course.

The greater part of all routine duties performed habitually by people every day is of this type. Consequently it does not belong in this classification, but also as will be shown later because its attachment to what are accustomed forms can be upheld with varying degrees of self-consciousness and in a variety of senses, in that case, the type may approach that of number two value-relatedness.

Strictly affectionate behavior also straddles the line of what may be considered meaningful oriented, and frequently it too crosses the line for instance; it may be an inhibited reaction to some extraordinary stimulus. It is a case of sublimation when effectually conditioned behavior issues in the form of conscious release of emotional tensions. When this happens it is usually, though not always, well on its way either toward value-related or goal oriented rational conduct or both.

Value-related conduct is distinguished from affectual conduct by its conscious formulation of the ultimate values government such conduct and its consistent planned orientation to these two types share in the fact that the meaning of the conduct does not lie in the achievement of some goal ulterior to it., but in engaging in the specific type of behavior for its own sake. Affectionately determined behavior is the kind which demands the immediate satisfaction of an impulse, regardless of how sublime or sordid it may be, in order to obtain revenge, sensual gratification complete surrender to a person or ideal blissful contemplation, or finally to release emotional tensions.

Examples of pure related conduct would be the behavior of persons who regardless of the consequences conduct themselves in such a way as to put into practice their honor, beauty religiosity, piety or the important of a cause no matter what it goal.

Within our terminology such value-related behavior is always pursuant to command the person engaging in it to constitute an obligation for him. Only insofar as human conduct is oriented exclusively toward such unconditional demand and this is true to a very modest degree will it be considered as value-related, i.e. oriented toward absolute values.

It will be that this type of conduct is important enough to justify it is being singled out, a special type though it should be noted that no attempt is made here to formulate in anyway exhaustive classification of certain types of behavior.

Ration conduct is of the goal-oriented kind when it is engaged in with due consideration for end means, and secondary effects, such conduct must also weigh alternate choices, as well as the relations of the end to other possible uses of the means and finally, the relative importance of different possible. The classification of conduct either in affectionate or traditional terms is thus incompatible with these types.

The decision between competing and conflicting ends and results may in turn be determined by a consideration of absolute value in the case, such as conduct is goal-oriented only in respect to the choice of means. Or the person engaged in such conduct may, rather than decide between conflicting and competing ends in terms of value-related orientation merely take them as given subjective wants and arrange them on a scale in order of priority.

He may then orient his conduct according to this scale in such a way that it confirms as far as possible to the order of priority as prescribed by the principle of marginal utility. This value-oriented conduct can be variously related to goal-oriented conduct, from the point of view of the latter however, value-orientation acquires more irrationality the more absolute it becomes.

For, the more unconditionally the individual devotes himself to such value for its own sake be it because sentiment, beauty, absolute kindness, or devotion to duty the less is there any though of the consequences of such devotion. Absolute goal-oriented conduct (i.e.) pure expediency, without any reference to basic values is essentially only a constructive exception.

Barely is conduct, especially social conduct, oriented only in one or other of these ways. Nor does this represent an exhaustive classification of the types of conduct now existing it is meant merely to arrive at certain conceptually pure forms of sociologically closely approximated so important types, to which social conduct as is much more usual, which constitute the elements joining to make it up. Only its future success can justify the usefulness of this classification for the purpose of our investigation.

Human Being Relationships

Philosophy human beings are social creatures. At the time of creation, God said it was not good for human beings to be alone. He gave Adam a companion, instructed the human race to multiply, and has permitted us to expand into the billions of people who now occupy the planet earth.

Whether two or more of these people together, there are interpersonal relationships that are both mutually supportive and characterized by clear concise and efficient communication. Often, however, interpersonal relations are strained and marked by conflict. Modern men and woman take pride in their individualism, independence, and self-determination, but sometimes these traits cut us off from other people and make us more insensitive, lonely, and unable to get along with others.

We live in the formation age with its many multimedia and mechanical devices to aid communication and interaction, but we still misunderstand one another, fail to get along, and often feel isolated and alone.

Many years ago, psychiatrist Harry Stack Sullivan suggested that all personal growth and healing, as well as all personal damage and regression, come through relationships with other people. All counseling, and almost all the issues discussed in this book, deal directly or indirectly with impersonal relations.

How people get along with each other, including how they communicate must be an issue of crucial concern to all Christian counselors. The Bible records along human history interpersonal problems and communication breakdown. Adam and Eve, the first married couple, had a disagreement about the reason for their sin in the Garden of Eden.

Their first two sons had a conflict that led to murder. Then, as its population multiplied, the earth filled with violence. A few years after the flood, the herdsmen of Abram and Lot and began fighting, there were family disputes, and a whole succession of wars continued throughout Old Testament history. Things were not much better in New Testament times.

The disciples of Jesus argued among themselves about who would be the greatest in heaven. In the early church, Ananias and Sapphira lied to the fellow believers, Jesus and the Greeks were at odds with each other, and there were disputes over doctrine. Many times in his letters, the apostle Paul commented on the disunity of the church and appealed for peace.

In this own missionary activities he was involved in conflict, and one occasion wrote to the Corinthians expressing the fear that if he came to visit he night find quarreling. Jealousy, outbursts of anger faction, slander gossip arrogance disorder and other evidence of interpersonal tension and sin.

Although the Bible records many examples of dissension, such interpersonal strife is never condoned or overlooked. On the contrary, strife is strongly forbidden, and principles for good interpersonal relations are mentioned frequently. The book of Proverbs, for example, instructs us to hold our tongues and avoid slander, to tell the truth, to speak gently, to think before we talk, to listen carefully, to resist the temptation to gossip, to avoid flattery, and to trust in God.

Unrestrained anger, hasty word, personal pride, dishonesty, envy, the struggle for rich, and host of other harmful attributes are mentioned as sources of tension. There is no book in the Bible that equals Proverbs in clear, consistent teaching about good relationships between people.

The teaching, however, does occur elsewhere. Much of the Sermon on the mount concerns interpersonal relations. Throughout his later ministry Jesus taught about conflict resolution and intervened in several disputes. Paul warned Timothy not to be quarrelsome, especially over unimportant things. Other Bible passages offer instructions to live in harmony, to demonstrate love, and to replace bitterness and wrath with kindness, forgiveness, and tenderhearted action. After a warning against those who cause trouble because they do not control their tongues, James notes that quarrels and conflict come because of personal lust and envy. Then in the midest of an exciting list of practice guideliness for living, we read Paul's instructions to avoid revenge to not repay anyone evil for evil, and to make every effort to live in peace with everyone.

Jesus and the biblical writers were peacemakers who, by their example and exhortation, expected modern believers to be peacemakers as well. As we ponder the many biblical statements about interpersonal relations, several themes are apparent. Good interpersonal relations, several themes are apparent. The best interpersonal relations begin with Jesus Christ have been promised an inner supernaturally produced peace, that gives internal stability, even in times of turmoil and interpersonal tension.

Peace with God comes when we confess our sins, ask him to take control of our lives, and expert that he will give us the peace that the word of God promises. Why then do Christians so often appear to be in conflict with each other and with nonbelievers? Why do so many of us have trouble getting along?

Good interpersonal relations depend on personal traits. There is nothing wrong with negotiations between individuals in conflict, political factions protagonist in labor disputes or between nations such efforts at peace making often can be helpful, but the Bible puts greater emphasis on the attitudes and characteristics of the persons involved in the disputes, in the first letter to the Corinthians, Paul appears to divide people into three categories. The first of these are the non believing people, which are characterized by sexual immorality, debauchery involvement in occult practices, hatred, discord, jealousy uncontrolled anger, selfishness, ambition, dissensions, factions, envy and various failures in self control.

These people may desire and strive for peace, but their basic alienation from God makes both inner peace and interpersonal peace unattainable. The second group, known as worldly people, has committed their lives to Christ, but they have never grown spiritually. They act like nonbelievers and often resort to jealousy and quarrelling. Since many church members appear to be in this group, we have the sad spectacle of believers in conflict, sometimes in violent conflict, with their neighbors and with each other. Some of these worldly Christians read the Bible regularly and have a good understanding of theology, but their beliefs mostly are intellectual and seem to have had little influence in their lives interpersonal relationship.

In contrast, spiritual people, the third group, are Christians who are yielded to divine control and are seeking to think and live with Christ. Sometimes these people slip into their former worldly ways and actions, but often their lives show increasing evidence of the fruits of the spirit that involve love, joy, peace, patience, kindness, goodness, faithfulness, gentleness, and self control. When people are transformed within a slow process of change begins in their outward behavior.

Christian's counselors can remember an important principle for real peace to be felt within or to occur individuals there must first be peace with God. This comes when individuals commit their lives to Christ, have regular times of worship, prayer and meditation on God's word, followed by changed thoughts and actions. Good interpersonal relations involve determination, effort and skill.

The great interpersonal relations do not always happen automatically, even among committed Christians. The Bible and psychology agree that good relationships depend on the consistent development and application of skills such as listening, watching, understanding oneself and others, refraining from comments or emotional outbursts and communicating accurately. All of this is learned; all of it can be taught by a perceptive Christian counselor. Christianity is a religion of relationship. Its founder is the god of love and is its most distinguishing characteristic.

This is not a powerful, sacrificial, giving love that involves the characteristics described in 1 Corinthians 13 and reflects the love of God who sent his son to die for individuals in a sinful world. The church is failing in its duty if it does not preach and practice this love that is so central to the Christian message.

Whenever such a message is preached and practiced, interpersonal tensions reduce. God has also given some more specific guidelines for showing this love. Much advice is given in the page of the Bible and in addition he has allowed us to discover additional principles for getting along and communicating effectively interpersonal relationships can improve and many interpersonal tensions can be prevented when people of all ages are taught and encouraged to practice consistently. Human beings are complex creatures with individual personalities and strong will. We are crowded on a planet that seems to be over populated with individuals whose sinful natures put them at adds with God and with each other.

Many of us want to get along with others, but this is not easy, perhaps the apostle Paul was thinking like this when he wrote the following inspired directive. If it is possible, as far as it depends on you, live at peace with everyone. These words come near the end of a few paragraphs dealing with practical rules for getting along, love others sincerely, be devoted to one another in brotherly love, honor one another above yourselves, share with others, be willing to associate, live in harmony with others, be willing to associate with people of low position, do not be conceited, do not pay back evil for evil, do what is right in the eyes of everyone. Surely it is interesting that the instruction to live in peace is preceded by two qualifiers: if it is possible and as far as it depends on you.

The first of these implies that sometimes it is not possible to live in harmony with others. Even so, each person has the responsibility for his or her own attitudes and behavior. As much as it depends on each of us, we are to live in peace. With the help of the Holy Spirit, Christian counselors try to establish such peace and prevent the strain that is characteristics of so many interpersonal relationships.

Marriage Partner

In philosophy, Christians would agree that the most important decision in life is whether to accept or reject Jesus Christ as one's savior and Lord. Second only to this is the choice of a life partner. In some cultures the decision is easy.

Marriages are arranged by the parents or families who sometimes enlist the aid of a marriage kroker. This professional match-maker considers family histories and proceeds to negotiate the best exchange in terms of bride piece or dowry. The young couple may have no say in the matter and may not even meet each other until the day of the marriage. How different this is from our society. For many marriages is no longer considered sacred or permanent. Living together out of wedlock entering marriages casually and dissolving marriage freely are all accepted parts of the western way of life.

For many people the careful choice of a life partner and the commitment to live with one's chosen mate for better or for worse have been replaced with a self-centered attitude that see marriage as a convenient living arrangement that can always be terminated if love grows cold.

Christians, in contrast, still acknowledge the permanence of marriage at least in theory if not in practice. Divorce, while common, is not encouraged, and single people take the choice of a mate very seriously. Some religious groups teach that God has one special person for each of us and that it is important not to miss God's best for your life. This attitude creates great anxiety in young people who are never told how to be sure if a choice is right, but who fear they might be sinning and missing God's blessing if one's choice is wrong. The problem is complicated when parents are led to believe that one person is the divinely chosen mate but the young person feels God leading in a different direction. In attempting to choose a mate wisely, many unmarried people seek guidance from a friend, older couple, Pastor or professional counselor. Books on counseling tend to overlook this subject, but helping another person in the choice of a life partner can be one of the counselor's most fulfilling tasks.

But, the Bible says little about mate selection. Jesus gave his sanction to marriage and so did Apostle Paul or neither discussed how a marriage partner should be established. This silence may reflect the fact that in biblical times choosing a mate was not a responsibility for the couple. For example, the choice of a wife for Isaac. His father sent a servant on a long journey to find a suitable candidate. The servant sought divine guidance in this process, and God gave a sign from heaven. When Rebekah was chosen, her parents were consulted and they asked the girl if she was willing to leave her family (perhaps forever) and travel to marry a man whom she had never met. Nobody even talked about love or dating. Everybody assumed that the lord was guiding in the choice, but personality, compatibility, sexual attraction, love, or the bride and groom's preferences were not part of the decision-making process.

With Jacob the situation was different. He was away from his parents when he fell in love, so the groom went directly to Rachel's father, although not to the bride Isaac and Jacob married later in life, but apparently many people in biblical times married young sometimes as early as age twelve or thirteen. The parents usually made the decision, just as they do in parts of the world today, but the young person could make his or her wishes known and sometimes even refuse to go along with the parental choice.

After a marriage had been arranged, there often was a period of unbreakable betrothal or engagement followed by a ceremony of marriage. It appears that sometimes the groom did not even see the bride's face until they were in bed together after the marriage. Even the thought of such a prospect can send shivers of anxiety up and down the spines of most contemporary single people. Do we have biblical guidelines for choosing a mate today? Some have suggested that there is only one—believers are to marry only other believers; the Christian should not marry a non-Christian. Do not be yoked together with unbelievers, Apostle Paul wrote. For what do righteousness and wickedness have in common.

What has the believer in common with the unbeliever? This is a warning: the Christian and non-Christian cannot pull together either as business partners or as marriage partners. A similar idea is emphasized in 1 Corinthians 6 and specifically applied to marriage when Paul states that the unmarried woman is free to marry whomever she wishes but only if marries a Christian.

What about divine guidance? Just as Abraham's servant expected and experienced divine leading in selecting a wife for Isaac, perhaps most Christians would agree that we still can expect God's leading in mate selection. In writing about marriage, Paul instructed his readers to be sure that you are living as God intended, marrying or not marrying in accordance with God's direction and help. This may apply more to general lifestyle than to mate selection, but several other biblical passages teach that believers can expect divine leading even though this may not come in dramatic or seemingly miraculously ways. Christians are divided over the issue of whether God has only one choice for a person who is seeking a life partner. In his controversial and widely discussed book, *"Decision Making and the Will of God,"* Gary Friesen argues convincingly that there is no biblical support for the idea that in all the universe God has only one person for each of us, that the identity of this person will be revealed in time, and that life will be miserable if you marry someone else.

According to scriptural teachings, Friesen writes marriage and singleness are both acceptable to God and the choice of a mate is governed only by the requirement that Christians must marry Christians. Beyond that Christians are free to choose a marriage partner based on one's own careful thinking and the thoughtful input of other sensitive people, including a Christian counselor. Considering or choosing a marriage partner has been called one of the most rewarding of all the choices in life, it is also one of the most difficult. Many people appear to make unwise choices and their lives, as a result, are miserable.

Because of this, some people are afraid or unwilling to take the risks of choosing a mate and building a marriage. To help people choose wisely and lessen the risk of making a mistake, counselors might consider answers to five important questions.

1. Why do people choose a marriage partner?

Some might answer that most people marry because they are in love. Love may be one of the most confessing ambiguous words in the English language. To fall in love is to feel an exhilarating, exciting closeness and intimacy with another human being. This emotional high, however, cannot last by itself forever. For deep love to pursuit and grow there must be a giving, other-centered relationship similar to that described in 1 Corinthians 13.

It may be that for most people deep and secure love comes after marriage rather than before. To be in love, therefore, is to experience a state of emotional exhilaration, to grow in love is to involve oneself deliberately in acts of giving and caring. A feeling of being in love is not in itself a solid basis for marriage (and neither is the fact that we do not love each other anymore a basis for divorce). The biblical marriages, like marriage in many countries today, were based on issues other than feeling, and even in our society it is probable that people really marry for reasons other than love. These reasons may be diverse, but often they center around the idea of needs. One theory of mate selection, for example, claims that opposites attract and that single people are drawn to potential partners who can meet one's needs by supplementing one's area of weakness. A dominant person, therefore, might be attracted to someone who is less dominant, or an introvert may choose a person who is extroverted.

More accepted is the broader view marriage meets mutual needs for companionship, security, support, intimacy, and sexual fulfillment. In addition, some marry because of premarital pregnancy, a yielding to social pressure, the desire to escape from an unhappy home environment, a fear that one will be left alone, a rebound reaction to the breakup of a prior engagement, or a compulsion to rescue some unfortunate single person. Each of these reasons for marriage meets some need, although none in itself can be the basis for a mature and stable relationship. Perhaps you have noticed that some of these reasons for selecting a mate are immature and self-centered; others are more rational and may result from mutual deliberation and respect. In all of this it is wise to remember that people marry, ultimately, because God created us male and female, instituted marriage for companionship, mutual support, and sexual expression, and declared in his word that marriage is honorable. This must not be forgotten as we help people struggle through the choice of a marriage partner.

1. Why do some people not choose a marriage partner?

The same God who created marriage apparently did not expect that everyone would find a mate. Jesus never had a wife. An unmarried Paul wrote that singleness should be considered a superior state since the unmarried person can be free for undistracted devotion to the Lord. Some people remain single, therefore, because they believe that this is the will and calling of God for their lives.

There are other, probably more common reasons why some people do not marry. First, there is the failure to meet an eligible partner. Since there are more women than men, it follows that there simply are not enough potential husbands to go around. In addition most people want a mate who has similar interests or education, but many people who desire marriage may not be able to find such compatible prospects. Consider, for example, the believer who wants a Christian mate but lives in an area where there are few eligible Christians. The desire for marriage may be perfect and stronger, but the prospect is not.

Second, some people fail to take advantage of the opportunities that are present. Busy with education, building a career, travel, or other activities, these people decide to postpone marriage and eventually the prospective disappears. Others, with high expectations, keep waiting for someone better and discover too late that they have passed by some excellent opportunities for marriage.

There is always hope, suggested one women in a somewhat humorous article. The key for finding a mate, she wrote, is to drop your notions of finding Mr. Right who will solve all your problems. One forty-two year old woman, for example, after many years of searching for the right man, finally wound up with a shy, sweet, loving fellow who made her very sweet, loving fellow who made her very happy but was far from her usual dynamic, intellectual charmer type. The lady listed the characteristics she wanted in a husband and then broke her list into four categories in declining order of importance: What I can't live without, absolute musts, extremely important trait, and what would be nice to have. Then she dropped the last three categories and cut the first in half. Not everybody is this anxious to find a mate.

Even if they write down lists of desirable traits for a mate, people in a third categories still remain single because they are unattractive to those of the opposite sex. This may result from mental or physical defects, but more often psychological characteristics drive others away. People who are excessively timid, afraid of the opposite sex, too aggressive or loud, insensitive, socially inappropriate in their dress and mannerisms, or self-centered often cannot relate well in dating. The individual who is overly concerned about getting married can also scare off and drive away potential mates.

Fourth, there is a failure of some people to achieve emotional independence. An unusually strong dependence upon one's parents or guilt over leaving a parent can cause some to remain single. In addition, there are responsible people who make a mature and deliberate choice to remain single because of a duty to care for needy family members. Sometimes, however, this can be an excuse to keep from taking the risks involved in entering a marriage and building intimacy.

Fifth, some people prefer to find intimacy apart from traditional marriage. Living together secretly or openly in what used to be called common-law marriages, joining a commune, participating in a trial marriage or group marriage, or forming a homosexual relationship are alternatives to marriage that lead some people to remain single.

Finally, some persons simply do not want to marry. This group includes homosexuals, those who have been burned in previous relationships and people who are afraid of the opposite sex, of sexual relationships, of intimacy, and/or of losing independence. Then there are others, mature, well-adjusted people, who decide that they would prefer to remain single in spite of social pressures that might push them toward marriage.

1. Where do people find mates?

Several decades of research have confirmed that most people select mates from similar social classes, economic and educational levels, occupations, age groups, race, religious backgrounds, and areas of residence. People often cross some of these barriers, of course, and many are able to build successful marriage despite their different background. Crossovers can also bring pressure that makes marital adjustment more difficult. Within recent years, for example, increasing numbers of women have been marrying younger men. Often there are good relationships except for the issue of children.

Older women tend to be involved in careers and are less willing to have children; their husbands, however, are more inclined to want families. This can create tension in looking for a mate; therefore, most people try to find someone who is of similar background and social-religious-educational level. Within this broad category the choice is often narrowed by one's personal standards, parental approval or disapproval, and by the single person's mental image of an ideal mate.

Since few people can measure up to these great expectations, there often must be a relaxing of one's standards a willingness to accept the less desirable characteristic in a potential mate, or a decision to remain single until the ideal person comes along. All of this background age, socioeconomic and educational level, parental and personal expectations—resides in the minds of single people who contemplate marriage.

With the entire opposite-sex population of single people thus narrowed, the unmarried person keeps alert to the people who are seen, met, or befriended at school, work, church, social and athletic gatherings, conferences, or in the neighborhood. It is well known that one person often may be attracted to another who has no desire to respond romantically. Sometimes a couple will meet first as friends or work associates with no thought of marriage, but then a more personal relationship begins to build. Other relationships start with feelings of sexual attraction, but before there can be a successful marriage, the couple must discover at least some similarities in their viewpoints and a mutual ability to meet each other's needs. For the Christian there is, in addition, the absolute essential that the two persons are believers.

1   Why do some people choose unwisely?

Although choosing a mate is one of life's most important decisions rarely is it done in a logical analytical manner? Subtle influences, parental and society pressures or unconscious desires, often edge people into relationships that may be unhealthy. In addition some people may have unrealistic expectations about how their needs night be met in marriage. Several year ago a survey attempted to discover what unmarried people were hoping for in a marriage. This list might be different if the survey could be repeated today, but perhaps many people still hope to find someone to love me, confide in, show affection, respect my ideals, appreciate what I wish to achieve, understand my moods, help make my decisions, stimulate my ambition, look up to, give me self-confidence, back me in difficulty, appreciate me just as I am, admire my abilities, make me feel important, and relieve my loneliness. While each of these is realistic and most are found in mature marriages, the satisfaction of these needs only comes when each mate gives to the other.

When single people choose a mate solely on the basic of what one can receive from marriage, they are preparing for future marital tension. This lopsided desire to receive without giving is a mark of immaturity and sometimes of neurosis. Other issues that reflect immaturity and lead to unwise marital decisions are a desire to prove one's adulthood, to escape from a difficult home situation to rebel against parents or a former partner, to escape the stigma of being single, to find a substitute for a previous relationship; marrying on the rebound to get a sexual partner, to improve one's economic-social status, or to bolster one's self-esteem and masculinity or femininity.

Other circumstances that warrant special caution and signal possible difficulties include wide age differences, recent mental illness in one or both individuals, no evidence of financial security, serious drug involvement, a pregnant bride, divergent religious traditions wide cultural or obvious racial differences, or participants who have never dated anyone other than the intended mate. Good marriage can occur despite these obstacles, but when several are present or when a couple appears to have unhealthy motives for choosing a mate; the choice is likely to be regretted later.

1. Why do some people choose wisely?

Despite all of the potential for failure, some people make a wise choice of a marriage partner. What are the reasons for this? A) Christian convictions. In western cultures, most mates are known first through dating. Since one never knows when a dating relationship may lead to marriage, it is a wise policy for unmarried Christian persons to limit their dating to other believers. Christians who choose wisely often pray about mate selection, at first alone and later as a couple.

B) Similar backgrounds and complementary needs. Christians, like nonbelievers, are unique and at different levels of emotional maturity. It does not fulfill and stable simply because both people are followers of Jesus Christ. As we have indicated, marriage selection is best when the man and woman are similar in variables such as age, interest, values, socioeconomic level, and education. In addition, it is helpful if the couple can meet each other's needs. Try, however, to distinguish between complementary and contradictory needs. Complementary needs fit so well together that a relationship is smooth and compromise is rarely needed. Contradictory needs clash and require frequent resolution. If both people enjoy social contacts but one person is outgoing and the other is a little shy, this can be complementary. In contrast, if one person loves parties and the other prefers to remain at home, these contradictory needs make conflict almost inevitable. C) Emotional resonance. As single people many of us have had the experience of asking, "How can I know when the right one comes along?" To hear someone reply, you will just know it is a common but not very satisfying answer. Some relationships are felt to be harmonious and right. With others, the spark just isn't there.

To choose a mate on the basis of such feeling alone would surely be unwise, but to ignore one's feelings or to overlook the fact that there are no feelings of attraction would also be a mistake. D) Marriage ability traits. In his creative theory of marriage personalities, Christian counselor David Field identified seven characteristics that appear in healthy marriage: time spent together, mutual spiritual interests, negotiating ability, maturity, play and humor, intimacy (including expressions of appreciation and the sharing of inner thoughts and feelings), and the willingness to make commitments.

When characteristics such as these are present before marriage, it seems likely that there will be wiser mate selection and subsequently greater marital satisfaction and stability. Other traits that could contribute to wise mate selection might include:

adaptability and flexibility, the ability and willingness of persons to adjust to change, to accept differences in a partner, and to adapt if necessary.

Empathy a sensitivity to the hurt and needs of others and a willing attempt to see and experience the world from the other person's perspective. The ability to work through problems, the recognition of emotions, and a willingness to define the issues and work toward solutions. The ability to give and receive love elements that are both necessary. Emotional stability accepting one's emotions, controlling them, and expressing them without tearing down another person. Communication ability—learning to talk frequently to one another about a wide range of subjects, to convey the feeling that one understands and is sensitive to the other, to keep communication opportunities open, and to express oneself personally, clearly, and at times nonverbally.

Commitment—the willingness to yield oneself to a lifetime of adventure including the risks, joys, and sorrows, plus a commitment to work together even when difficulties, obstacles, and challenges interfere with a smooth relationship. Counselors and single people can be discouraged when they see lists like these. Almost nobody can meet all of these expectations. The lists show, however, that for mate selection, a feeling of love or a strong urge to get married cannot be the sole basis for making a wise choice. The outside perspective and guidance of a friend or counselor can be helpful and important if one is to attain subsequent marital stability and happiness. But, good choices do not always lead to good marriage, but careful selection of a mate does give a solid foundation on which to build a husband-wife relationship.

Marriage involves effort, risk, and sometimes disappointment. These are never easy experiences, but it is more pleasant and motivating to work with a compatible teammate in life than with someone who apparently was the wrong choice. Many people, however, make choices that in retrospect seems to have been unwise, but the couple determines nevertheless to build the best relationship possible considering the circumstances. These people discover that loving actions often create loving feelings. In time relatively good marriages can result in contrast other people never recover from poor mate selection. Unhappiness and conflict characterize the marriage and the relationship is dissolved emotionally if not legally through separation and divorce. Counseling people in the selection of a marriage partner has the goal of preventing such unhappy endings to marriage.

Despite its importance, the selection of a marriage partner is seldom done carefully, objectively, and rationally. When people fall in love they tend to overlook the faults in each other, to ignore danger signals, and to dismiss the counsel of more objective persons. Few are likely to come for counsel until after a potential mate has been chosen, and most do not even come then. The counselor's help is most likely to come through informal talks with young people before they fall in love, through devotionals and other public speaking to singles groups, through side discussions with counselees who have come to get help for other problems; or through counseling with the never married and formerly married who come for help in evaluating the wisdom of their mate choices. There are several goals for this counseling, goals that apply equally to young unmarried persons and to older individuals, including widows and divorced persons, who would like to get married or remarried.

1. Spiritual Evaluation. Since the Bible is so clear in its teaching that believers should marry only believers, this must be emphasized repeatedly. Even when they believe this, people often look for excuses to justify their dating of non-Christians. We do not plan to get serious, they say, or if we date it could lead my friend to Christ. Statements like this usually are made with sincerity, but they signal a sidestepping of biblical teaching about the unequal yoke. Although Christians sometimes do lead potential mates to Christ, the reverse is also true and perhaps more likely nonbelievers cause Christians to stumble spiritual or to lose spiritual vitality.

This needs to be stated clearly at some time in counseling. Dating nonbelievers is risky and in general should be avoided.

When a potential marriage partner is being considered, encourage the counselee to ask questions such as the following and suggest that the answers be discussed with the counselor. Is my potential mate a believer? Does his or her life show evidence of the fruits of the spirit (Gal 5:22-23)? Have my partner and I ever discussed our spiritual lives, struggles, and goals? Have we ever prayed together? If not, why not? Do we agree on a church, on our basic standard of living on our views about right and wrong, and on our perspectives about a Christian home?

1. Reassurance. Sometimes people come to a counselor with the fear that they never will get married. They may wonder if something is wrong or if God married. Encourage these people to admit and express their feelings, including feelings of anger and frustration and give the reassurance that God always cares and wants the best for us. Openly discuss the realities and discouragement of the single life. But point out too that singleness can be a special calling. Is the counselor willing to remain single? If not, why not? By observing and by asking, try to determine: a) if the person shows traits (like over-eagerness, timidity, or insensitivity) that may be driving away members of the opposite sex and b) if the counselee's life is so bound up in the desire to marry that little else seems to matter. Many people live in the future. They assume that life will be better when they earn more money, graduate from college, get a better job, or find a mate. While they wait, their lives are largely meaningless,

nonproductive, and stagnant. Such people should be encouraged to live life to the fullest now. If a mate is found, this will be great. If no mate is found, life can also be worthwhile and fulfilling.

1. Giving direction in mate selection. Some people need practical guidance in finding eligible partners. This involves two issues; finding places where there are other single people and learning how to relate. It is an obvious but frequently overlooked fact that one does not find a mate by sitting at home watching television and waiting for God's gift of marriage to arrive at the door. To meet people, including potential marriage partners, one must go where others are. For some this means singles bars, but for many people, including believers, this is not considered a suitable place to find a mate. More desirable are churches, study courses, vacation trips, sports events, Christian single adult groups, and Christian conferences.

Yet if one goes to these places primarily to find a marriage partner, this soon becomes apparent to everyone. Nothing drives people away like a single person's overanxions desire to lateh onto potential mates. It is better to get involved in groups that are interesting; knowing that in so doing one may or may not find a potential partner. Sometimes counselees may need to be reminded that they should look neat and attractive, learn how to ask questions about others, and try to be good listeners to who are interested in other people. It is important to be oneself instead of pretending to be something we are not. The counselor can gently point out failings in these areas and, if necessary, do some role playing in which the counselor and counselee pretend to be strangers so they can practice relating to one another

4) Evaluating motives, ideals, and maturity. Why does the counselee want to find a mate or why does he or she not want to marry? The counselee's answers to these questions sometimes are not what counselors expect. It can be helpful, therefore, to ask why do you want to get married. Try to determine, sometimes by raising tentative questions, if these are unhealthy reasons for wanting marriage like social and families pressures, the desire to escape an unpleasant home situation, the need to prove that one is an adult, or the feeling that marriage is now or never.

If the person has chosen to remain single, ask yourself if there are also unhealthy reasons for this, is there a fear of marriage, of sex, or of the opposite sex? Is the person homosexual? Is he or she rebelling against something, including traditional forms of marriage? Ask the counselee to discuss these attitudes. Talk about their implication and the possible reasons for their presence. If his is a desire for change, discuss how this might be done. Try to focus attention on specific issues and talk about how the counselee could take action to change. At some point it may be god to ask a counselee to describe his or her ideal mate. Then discuss this expectation. Is it unrealistic, is it causing the counselee to overlook or reject potentially good marriage partners who do not fit the ideal? Can part of the ideal be changed without lessening one's moral standards? As these issues are discussed, try to assess the counselee's level of maturity.

Immature single people make immature marriage partners and this can lead to problems in dating and marriage. The spiritually maturing Christian shows a desire to be like Christ, accompanied by some evidence of the fruits of the spirit in his or her life. In counseling you may want to discuss some of these issues. In which does the person succeed and where does he or she fail? How could these traits and attitudes be developed? The more of these that are present, the greater the likelihood of successful mate selection and marital stability.

5) Teaching about mate selection. In many respect, counseling is a specialized form of education. Now here is this more true than when one is helped to choose a mate. Earlier we discussed the reasons why some people choose wisely. The contents of that section could be shared with the counselee, but it may be best to do this slowly and at different times throughout counseling. In this way, the counselee is not overwhelmed with information that may not be easy to handle.

6) Encouraging patience. In all of this, encourage counselees to be patient, to pray regularly about a marriage partner, to trust

in God's leading and timing, and to be alert for opportunities to meet potential mates. Pray for and with counselees, asking for patience, for purity and protection for both the counselee and his or her potential mate, and for the willingness to accept singleness joyfully if this is God's plan. In the selection of a marriage partner, to be forewarned is the best protection against mistakes. Information from the first parts of this chapter could be presented to singles privately or to singles groups, Sunday school classes, youth groups, special interest groups, or weekend conferences. If this or similar material is presented, be sure that there is opportunity for people to discuss what they hear, to ask questions, and to ponder how in practical ways this learning can be applied to their own lives. The sooner such information is presented and discussed, the better. As we have noted, facts about mate selection tend to lose significance and influence after one has fallen in love. If facts and warning can be given before emotional bonds are allowed to develop, it is more likely that error will be avoided. Thus single people should learn to evaluate relationships intellectually. This could steer them away from potentially harmful involvements before getting into a situation where they might fall romantically and emotionally in love. When all of this is understood and practiced, much progress has been made toward the prevention of poor mate selection. With some counselees, prevention will start long before a prospective mate appears. Immature or self-centered people, for example, can often profit from individual or group counseling that helps them cope more effectively with life in general. This can remove some of the unhealthy attitudes and behavior that can lead to an unwise selection of a marriage partner. Our whole culture on an appetite for buying, on the idea of mutually favorable exchange. Modern man's happiness consist of looking at shop windows, and in buying all that he can afford to buy either for cash or on installments. He or she looks at people in a similar way. For the man an attractive girl and for the women an attractive man is the prize they are after. Attractive usually means a nice package of qualities which are popular and sought after on the personality market. What specifically makes a person attractive depends on the fashion of the time physically as well as mentally.

During the twenties, a drinking and smoking girl tough and sexy was attractive. Today the fashion demands more domesticity and coyness. At the end of the nineteenth and the beginning of this century, a man had to be aggressive and ambitious. Today he has to be social and tolerant in order to be an attractive package. At any rate, the sense of falling in love develops usually only with regard to such human commodities as are within reach of one's own possibilities for exchange. I am out for a bargain; the object should be desirable from the standpoint of its social value and at the same time should want me, considering my overt and hidden assets and potentialities. Two persons thus fall in love when they feel they have found the best object available on the market, considering the limitations of their own exchange values. This is blunt humanistic analysis, but it contains an element of truth. Striking a marriage bargain may be more overt in other cultures where bride prices a part of a deal, but it surely is true that mate selection in out culture also includes some exchanges. The Christian recognizes, however, that marriage involves more. It is the joining of two individuals so they become one and yet remain unique and interlocking personalities. Probably it is untrue that within this world there is only one perfect God ordained person for each of us, but it surely is true that God can and often does lead individuals to marriage partners who will meet their needs and with whom they can blend their lives. Often he leads through counselors who are willing to give guidance as single people make the choice of a mate.

Marital Difficulties

Probably, marriage is not a very stable institution at least in the Western world. In the United States, the average duration of a marriage is 9.4 years. More than a million couples are divorced every year. Many who stay together have marriages like that of curt tolerable but not especially happy. In our efforts to help troubled relationships we sometimes forget that many people do have lasting and mutually satisfying marriages. Researchers recently surveyed three hundred couples who have been married for at least twenty years and who described themselves as happily married. The respondents show remarkable agreement in their views of what makes a marriage happy. Most frequently mentioned was having generally positive attitude toward one's spouse and viewing the partner as one's best friend.

In essence the couples said, I am married to someone who cares about me, who is concerned for my well being, who gives as much or more then he or she gets, who is open and trustworthy and who is not mired down in a somber, bleak outlook on life. The second key to successful marriage is a belief in the importance of commitment. Marriage is viewed as something people should stick with and work to develop in spite of difficult times.

In addition, happily married people believed about aims and goals in life, had a desire to make the marriages succeed, and were able to laugh a lot. To the researcher's surprise, fewer than 10% of the happily married people mention good sexual relations as an important ingredient for good marriages. Even though happy marriages like these do exist and are possible, we live in a time when marital unhappiness is more common where many see divorce as a convenient and ever present fire escape should marital conflicts get to hot to handle. Irreconcilable differences become reasons for marriage breakups, and no fault divorce allows marriage to be terminated legally when one or both spouses simply lose any desire to stay together. Marriage, the permanent union created by God, is treated more and more as a temporary arrangement of convenience. These social attitudes, coupled with the stresses that put pressure on modern marriages, often create problem that come to the counselor's attention.

Research during the past several years has shown consistently that more people seek counseling for marital problems than for any other single issue. It is not easy to help couples resolve marital conflicts and build better marriages, but this can be one of the most rewarding of all counseling experiences. In the Bible, marriage problems are one of the first topics discussed. It is mentioned throughout the page of scripture and considered in depth in the New Testament. The purposes of marriage, the roles of husband and wife, the importance of sex, and the responsibilities of parents are all discussed, sometimes more than once. Marriage failure is mentioned in the Old Testament law and treated in more detail by Jesus and Paul in their discussions of divorce.

What does the Bible say about marital problems and ways to help troubled marriages? Almost nothing; believers are encouraged to enjoy interpersonal and sexual relationships within their spouses, and finding a mate is described as a good thing. In contrast, the Book of Proverbs picturesquely decries the difficulties of living with a contentious quarrelsome marriage partner. Sharing a house with such a person is like listening to a constant dripping on a rainy day. Trying to control such a person is as futile as restraining the wind or grasping oil with the hand.

Although the Bible describes some good marriages, there is evidence that Lot, Abraham, Jacob, Job, Samson, David, and a numbers of others had marital tensions at least periodically. These are acknowledged honestly, but marital problems by people are not analyzed. It should be remembered that marital conflict often is a symptom of something deeper, such as selfishness, lack of love, unwillingness to forgive anger, bitterness, communication problems, anxiety, sexual abuse drunkenness, feelings of inferiority sin, and a deliberate rejection of God's will. Each of these can cause marital tension, each can be influenced by husband-wife conflict, and each is discussed in the Bible. Thus while the scriptures deal with marital conflict only indirectly and in passing, the issues underlying marriage problems are considered in detail. Many of these issues are discussed elsewhere in this book.

The causes ethics of marital difficulties, in Gen. 2:24, we read that in marriage a man will leave his father and will be united to his wife, and they will become one flesh. These verbs in this verse leaving being united, and becoming one indicate three purposes of marriage. Living involves a departure from parents and implies a public and legal union of husband and wife into a marriage. Walter Trobisch once wrote that couples that ignore this legal element have a stolen marriage. There are many reasons to be loved, sex, but they have no real reasons to give themselves to responsible marriage building.

Being united comes from a Hebrew word that means to stick or glue together. If you try a separate two pieces of paper which are glued together, both are hurt. Ideally the couple is dedicated to loving, drawing together and remaining faithful to each other.

When such uniting is absent, they have an empty marriage that may be legal but is devoid of love. Becoming one involves sex, but it goes beyond the physical. It means, writes Trobisch, that two persons share everything they have, not only their bodies, but only there material possessions, but also their thinking and feelings, there joy and suffering, there hopes and their fears, and their successes and failures.

This does not imply that two personalities squelched or obliterated. The uniquenesses remain but they are combined with those of one's mate to make a complete relationship. When the one flesh relationship is lacking the couple has an unfulfilled marriage. This kind of thinking is neither common nor popular today. People want happiness, the opportunity to realize one's potential, or having a full life but they fail to see that these contemporary and somewhat self-centered goals rarely come to marriages that ignore the biblical guidelines. Instead marital difficulties often arise because a husband and wife have deviated the biblical standards outlines in Gen. 2:24 and elaborated in later portions of scriptures. Modern psychology, sociology, and related disciplines have clarified some of the ways in which people deviate from these biblical standards for marriage.

In the professional literature, this is probably the most commonly mentioned cause of marital discord. Citing James 4:1-3, psychologist Lawrence Crabb notes that communication problems also come because individuals have not learned how to communicate clearly and efficiently. Communication involves the sending and receiving of messages. Messages are sent verbally and nonverbally with gestures, tone of voice, facial expressions, words on a piece of paper, image on the computer screen, action, gifts, or even periods of silence.

When the verbal and nonverbal contradict, a double message is sent. This leads to confusion and communication breakdown. Consider, for example, the woman who says verbally, "I don't mind if you go on the business trip", but whose slumping posture, resigned tone of voice, and depression-like lack of enthusiasm says, "I really don't want you to go." In contrast, a wife gets a confused double message when her husband says, "I love you and like spending time with you," but never is home, never takes his wife out to dinner, or never does anything to show his love and appreciation.

In good communication the message sent verbally is consistent with the message sent nonverbally. Good communication also demands that the message sent is the same as the message that is received. Assume, for example, that a man buys his wife a new dishwasher because he loves her. The wife, however, concludes that she isn't loved because her husband never says the words "I love you." She begins to wonder if the dishwasher was given because the husband feels guilty about something. Clearly there is miscommunication here because the message being sent love expressed by the gift of a dishwasher is not the message that is being received.

Most of us would agree that occasional miscommunication between spouses is inevitable. When miscommunication is more common than clear communication, however, the marriage begins to have serious problems. Poor communication tends to breed more of the same. Try to remember that communication is learned interaction. Even when it is not good, people can learn to make it better. Under-integrated, getting close to another person is risky. We open ourselves to criticism and possible rejection when we let another person know us intimately, become aware of our insecurities, or see our weakness. Since most of us have learned the value of fending for ourselves, it is not easy to trust another person even when the other person is a marriage partner.

In a book on stress management, one writer suggests that problem marriages tend to be under-integrated or over-integrated. In under-integrated marriage, the husband and wife appear to grow apart over the years. There is little willingness to share confidences, to be vulnerable, or to develop mutual life goals. Instead each seems to be moving through life independently of the other, with different needs and goals. There is a tendency to be defensive, to criticize and put down each other or to manipulate subtly.

Defensive, self-centered attitudes create tension and push the husband and wife apart. In contrast, over-integrated marriage occurs when a relationship has become so engulfing that both partners have lost their identities and feel trapped. If you suggest that one person's harshness may be creating marital difficulties; the response might be that right, but I'm not the only one who is guilty. Both partners blame the other for their problems and neither is able to stand back, look at individual needs, and evaluate one's own faults that may be contributing to the tension. In time there may be a verbal or physically violent reaction as both partners try to tear away from the confinement of such a stifling relationship. When two people marry, each comes to the marriage with approximately two or more decades of past experiences and ways of looking at life. Each has perspectives that are not shared by the other and sometimes, even when there is a sincere desire for compromise or synthesis, couples still has difficulty resolving their differences. What happens if there is unwillingness to change, too insensitive to the other person's viewpoints, or a refusal to acknowledge the differences? Often there is tension that frequently centers on one of the following issues. At times most couples have sexual problems. In an earlier chapter, we discussed some causes of sexual difficulties in marriage.

These include lack of accurate knowledge, unrealistic expectations, fear of not being able to perform adequately, differences in sexual drive, inhibiting attitudes about sex, and insufficient opportunities for privacy. Impatience, frigidity, and infidelity, perhaps the three most common sex problems, in turn create more tension, and this further hinders smooth sexual functioning.

Exceptional busyness, insensitivity in one or both of the partners, or nonsexual marital conflicts can also interfere with sexual functioning. When these problems are not resolved, marriage almost always suffers. Roles we live at the time when traditional male-female roles are being reevaluated. This often leads to conflict over what it means to be a husband or wife. The society gives little guidance because opinions seem to be changing so rapidly. The Bible, in contrast, is much more explicit, but Christians differ in their interpretations of the scriptural passages that outline husband-wife roles.

As a result there is disagreement, accompanied at times by both competition and feelings of threat. Often this tension centers on the nature and extent of the wife's work on goals. Inflexibility, when a man and woman marry, each brings a unique personality to the marriage. Sometimes these personality differences complement each other and blend into a mutually compatible relationship. Often marriages take on personalities of their own, each of which can have strengths and weak points.

There can be difficulties, however, if one or both of the partners is rigid, unwilling to give on strongly resistant to change. When a couple first marries there often is a time or excitement, enthusiasm, and youthful idealism. As the partners grow older and the months turn into years, the marriage must also change and mature if it is to stay healthy. According to Christian counselor H. Norman Wright, marriage must grow through stages if they are to remain stable and fulfilling.

When couples are too busy or too rigid to work at building and enriching their marriages, problems are likely to develop. Religion, the Bible warns of problems when a believer and an unbeliever try to live together in marriage. Counselors have observed tensions when a husband and wife differ from each other in their denominational preferences, degree of commitment to spiritual things, interest in religion, or expectations about the religious education of children.

Sometimes these difficulties create tension in other areas such as choice of friends, views of ethics, whether and to whom charitable donations will be given or the use of time on Sunday. Religion can be binding, strengthening force in a marriage, but when a husband and wife have different viewpoints, religion can also be a destructive focus for marital tension. What is really important in life? How should we spend our time and money? What are our goals? These questions concern values. When a couple has similar values, the marriage is often healthy and growing.

When values are in conflict, however, the relationship may be one of tension, power struggles, and mutual criticism. Value conflicts are at the heart of many marital problems. Consider, for example, how some of the following value alternatives could create potential for conflict.

1) Credit cards should never be used "verses" Credit cards can be used on occasion to get us over a financial crisis.

2) Divorce is never right "verses" Sometimes divorce is the best solution to marital problems.

3) Succeeding in one's career is of major importance in life "verses" Building a family is more important than building a career.

4) Children should be taught spiritual beliefs and values "verses" Children should be given the freedom to find their own beliefs.

5) We should never miss church on Sunday "verses" Sometimes it is ok to skip worship services.

Many of these views are held firmly. They influence how we act or relate to other people. In addition, values sometimes become the basis for intense conflict, especially if cherished beliefs are attached or challenged by one's mate.

Conflicting needs and personality differences. For almost a century psychologists have debated about the existence of human needs. Most agree that we each need food, rest, air, and freedom from pain, but there are also psychological needs such as the need for love, security, and contact with others. In addition, it seems that most people have unique personal needs such as the need to dominate, to control, to possess, to achieve or to help and rescue others. If one spouse has a need to dominate while the other wants to be controlled, then there may be compatibility.

If both husband and wife have a need to dominate, this creates potential for conflict. If both are devote to career building, there can be conflict, especially if one spouse wants to accept a career advancement that will involve a family move and the other spouse resists. Personality difference also can create tension. When one spouse is open freely sharing about one's needs, temptations, attitude, and feelings but the other spouse tends to hold things in these differences can create problems. One long-term study of sexual hundred marriages, researchers found that neurotic traits, especially impulsivity in the husband, frequently led to marital instability, distress, and divorce. Often these traits were noticed and ignored at the time of engagement, but they led to misery in the years that followed. Money, how are the family finances to be earned? How is it to be spent? What things are really needed and which are merely desirable? Is a budget necessary? How much should be given to the church? What happens when there is a shortage of money?

Answers to questions like these reflect one's financial values and attitudes. When a husband and wife have different answers to these kinds of questions, there is potential for conflict. Once again it is difficult to determine whether financial tensions cause other problems or whether the opposite is more accurate.

It is true however that a harmonious financial relationship is essential if there is to be a harmonious marriage. Sometimes marital tensions appear or are made worse because of the pressure that comes from other people or from stressful situations. These external sources of pressure include, in laws who criticize or otherwise make demands on the couple. Children whose needs presence often interfere with the depth and frequency of husband-wife contacts, and sometimes drive a wedge between the spouses. Financial reverses that put pressure on the family budget and lead to worry and sometimes disagreement about spending patterns.

Most of these pressures can be resisted but each can be a powerful threat to marital harmony. As the years go by, husbands and wives settle into routines, get accustomed to each other and sometimes slip into self-absorption, self-satisfaction or self pity, for each of which can drain any remain excitement from a marriage and make life boring. When marriage is dull and routine, couples sometimes begin to look elsewhere for variety and challenge. This turn creates further marital tension. These effects of marital difficulties: the bookstore and library shelves are filled with books describing the experiences of once happy marriages that grew cold, distant and unhappy. Even as they tell their own stories, the authors of these books show how difficult it can be can also lead to problems in bed or in balancing the checkbook. Although there is a circular relationship between cause and effect, the counselor can observe several specific effect of marital tension.

Every marriage is built on hope, suggests one Christian marriage counselor, people marry because they hope that life together will be more effective, satisfying, and purposeful than life alone. Nearly every marriage goes through periods of disillusionment. When this happens, hope is often replaced by sadness, hurt and anger. The partners feel hopeless, and hopeless feeling is contagious. One goal of counseling, therefore, must be the recovery of hope. It is impossible to estimate the number of people who are legally married, living together, and sometimes sleeping in the same bed, but who are emotionally and psychologically divorced. The husband and wife may even engage in similar activities and go places together, but there is little warmth, concern, communication, intimacy, love or interest in one's mate.

By withdrawing emotionally from each other, the partners avoid the pain and social stigma of divorce. Conflicts remain but there are few battlers, and the marriage persists as an uneasy trace that may extend a lifetime. When the marital and family pressures get too intense, some people simply leave. It is difficult to compile statistics on the incidence that thousands of mates desert their families each year and leave hurt feelings, confusion, uncertainty, financial pressures, and one-parent families behind. The courts can decree that a deserting spouse must return or meet family financial obligations, but these people lower-class families, the deserted mate often orders. Since most deserters are from lower-class families, the deserted mate often cannot afford the costs of bringing legal action against the spouse who has left.

Divorce might be viewed as the legal termination of a once-promising, hope-filled, and satisfying relationship that has been coming apart socially and emotionally. Even though it is common, divorce is never a happy solution to marital problems. It is used too often and too quickly as a way to escape marital difficulties. Even Christian couples sometimes ignore the biblical guidelines for dissolving a marriage. Nevertheless there are times when divorce may seem to be the most feasible alternative to a problem-plagued marriage.

Counseling one person is a difficult task; counseling a husband and wife is even more difficult and requires special skill and alertness in the counselor. Frequently one or both of the spouses come with skepticism about the value of counseling, and sometimes there is an attitude of resistance or hostility. Someone has called marriage counseling one of the most difficult and sensitive of therapies filled with psychological traps and surprises. Before starting and frequently thereafter counselors should look at themselves to clarify some of their own attitudes, prejudices, motivations and vulnerabilities.

What is your attitude toward marital problems? Are you critical of those who have marital difficulties, inclined to condemn, prone to take side, annoyed because these problems take so much time from your school, afraid that marital counseling might arouse anxieties about your own marriage? Are you nervous lest your counseling be a failure? Perhaps we need to remind ourselves that one's reputation as a counselor never rests on one case, even though there are literally hundreds of how-to-do it books and articles on marriage counseling, no one person can master all of the techniques. Your job is to be available to the couple, as technically skilled as possible, and sincerely willing to have the Holy Spirit work through you as an instrument of healing. Your help will be most effective if you can commit the counseling to God, relax, and try to provide an atmosphere where constructive discussion is possible.

In addition, try to understand both sides of the situation from the perspectives of the people involved. Intimate discussions about marriage can arouse sexual and other feelings in the counselor, feelings that must be admitted to oneself and handled often with the help of others. Sometimes a counselor will remind you of some person that you have known elsewhere. Unless you are alert and careful, your feelings and attitudes about this other person will become imposed on the counselees. This is hinder counseling. Be aware too that some counselees may cast you into a role that you may neither recognize nor want.

A woman, for example, might see her male counselor as a kind understanding man—so different from my insensitive, non-caring husband. The husband in return may think of the male counselor as a threat to the marriage and one who really doesn't understand the wife. In situations like these, try not to react in accordance with your feelings. Be careful not to let the counselee's expectations mold your behavior so that you overreact or become the kind of person that the counselee expected. When counselors have colleagues with whom they can discuss issues like these, the dangers are greatly reduced.

Within the past two or three decades, literally hundreds of marriage and family therapy techniques have been proposed and sometimes touted by enthusiastic advocates. Sculpting, for example, is a procedure where family members move around the room and position themselves in terms of how close or how far they feel from each other. Diagramming involves drawing a picture with the names of family members and other people set in boxes.

Then lines are drawn between the boxes to show how the different people relate. Solid lines, for example, may mean a good relationship, double lines mean a close relationship, a dotted line signifies a distant relationship, and a wavy line indicates conflict. Other counselors use role playing, drama, or even choreography in counseling. Unless you have special training in marriage counseling you may not wish to use these somewhat unusual techniques, but even if your approach is more traditional you are likely to discover that marriage counseling raises procedural questions that may not be present in other types of counseling. Should the couple be seen alone or together? Many counselors would say both. Sometimes, after an initial joint session, counselors will see the husband and wife separately for a few sessions. Often this gives new information and different perspectives on the problem. At times you will find that each spouse has a different opinion about what the major problem is and who is primarily responsible.

Sometimes you will discover that one of the partners wants counseling and the other does not. In some cases you will discover that one or both of the spouses have problems that will benefit from individual counseling. Marriage, however, is a relationship, and marital problems involve conflicts between two people. If these can be observed and discussed together sometimes with the children present, progress may be greater and faster whether you see the couple separately or together, be careful to strive for impartiality. Taking sides can often hinder your counseling effectiveness.

Should there be time limits for counseling? In his excellent book on Christian marriage counseling, psychologist Everett V. Worthington suggests three stages of counseling: assessment, intervention, and termination. At the beginning, Worthington asks the couple to agree to three sessions for assessment and evaluation of their difficulties. After that the couple and the counselor decide whether or not they should continue. If they continue, the counselor suggests that eight to sixteen sessions should be sufficient to complete the counseling intervention stage followed by termination. This is not a rigid approach, sometimes the counseling stops often a few sessions and at times it goes longer.

Within the past decade or two, however, there has been a strong movement in the counseling field toward short-term, time limited counseling. Increasing evidence suggests that the briefer approaches tend to be more effective than counseling that continues for months and years. In making you initial assessment, two issues are of great importance. First, try to discover where the couple is spiritually. Are they both believers? Are they growing spiritually or has religion become what William James once called "dull habit?"

The Christian counselor is likely to use different terminology and take more overtly Christian approach when it is clear that the husband and wife are believers. Second, be careful not to spend all of your initial time in discussing the problems. When they come for counseling a couple already feels defeated and well aware of the pain and conflict in their marriage. If the whole session is spent in a listing of problems, the counselees may feel so discouraged that they are reluctant to return for the next session.

Even as you gather information, therefore, remember that one of the main purposes of the early session is to build positive expectancies, establish a commitment for change, and begin the process of change. The counselor, the husband and wife each approach marriage counseling with expectations and goals. The goals may be either vague or clearly defined. Some will be realistic, others will not.

Some counselees will come with high expectations and a determination to work at healing the troubled marriage, others may have little hope or motivation to change, when the goals are clear, and accepted by everyone, marriage counseling starts with a high potential for success. When the goal are vague or in conflict, for example, the husband wants a smooth separation, but the wife wants a reconciliation, then counseling will be more difficult. What are your goals in counseling? When these are recognized clearly, counseling can be more effective, the counselor knows where he or she is going and with one's own goal in mind, it is easier to concentrate on the counselee goals and determine counselee goals. Sometimes the counselee's goals are similar to those of the counselor, but often there is a discrepancy. Questions like, "What would you hope to get out of counseling?", or "How would you like your marriage to be different?" often initiate discussion that clarifies, for the counselees as well as for the counselor what the husband and/or wife hope to achieve through counseling. One experienced counselor tries to determine the answers to four goal related questions as the counseling begins:

—How does each partner experience the
—Relationship?

    —What does each year for?
    —What can be done?
    —What is each partner willing to do now?

Acceptable goals many people have vague and distant goals, for example to have a Christian marriage, but these are reached best through a series of more specific, more attainable, more immediate goals. Some counselors work on a contract approach in which the husband and wife each agree to change behavior in some specific way during periods between counseling sessions. When a couple sets such goals with the counselor's help, there is increased motivation to attain these goals, and the couple can learn about communication and problem solving in the process. As goals are reached, the couple is encouraged because they see specific progress.

At times, however, there is disagreement about goals. Counselees sometime want help in attaining goals that the counselor considers unrealistic or immoral. If, for example, a wife complains that her husband has been unfaithful, but the husband wants the freedom to have occasional sexual contact during business trips, the Christian counselor is faced with a goal conflict. The counselor realizes the value of not taking sides, but the husband wants permission to continue behavior that clearly is sinful according to the Bible. In a non-condemning but honest way these differences in goals and values must be discussed. The counselor's goal is not to manipulate or force people to change, but neither should people be helped to act in ways that the counselor considers morally wrong, psychologically harmful, or detrimental to the marriage. If counselor-counselee goal conflicts persist, even often continued discussion, then withdrawal from the counseling and referral may be the best options.

If counselees have goals or values that differ from those of the counselor, or if the husband and wife have conflicting goals, all of this should be discussed openly. Usually there are at least some goals that everyone accepts, and it is possible to start there. Sometimes as counseling continues and as goals are clarified, the differences are not as divergent as they first appeared. The counselor must seek to understand people, their feelings, and their frustrations as well as we understand problems. Sometimes helpers are so intent on solving problems and finding ho-to-do it answers that they become insensitive to the pain and personalities of the people with whom they are working with. The basic counselor qualities of empathy, genuineness, and warmth are crucial in marriage counseling.

According to the dictionary, a process refers to the changes or continuous actions that are taking place during a period of time. In counseling, the word process often is used to describe the continuous ways in which people relate to each other or interact with the counselor during the counseling sessions. Carefully watch the couple as they interact with you and with each other in counseling. Listen to their descriptions of how the couple is relating, and then talk about ways that they could relate better. Are there different ways of relating that could be practiced between sessions? Be sure to discuss all of this when the couple returns.

Eventually, as you move toward termination, you may want to help counselees review what they have learned. Encourage them to launch out more and more on their own. Remind them that marriage counseling, like all other Christian counseling, is intended to help people grow personally, interpersonally, and spiritually. As counselors, our greatest successes come when couples learn to build marriages that are yielded to Jesus Christ based on biblical principles, characterized by a commitment to each other, and growing as the husband and wife constantly work at skillful communication, goal attainment, and conflict resolution.

Philosophy of the Bible, Christians believe that God, who created both male and female and who initiated marriage, also has given guidelines for marriage in the page of scripture. These guidelines need to be taught clearly at home and church and modeled consistently by Christian leaders. We live in a society that propagates non-biblical values about sex and marriage, so the biblical teachings about sex and the meaning of love need to be reinforced frequently.

Marriage enrichment and marital commitment. For most people life consists of a number of demands, commitments, and responsibilities. Often in the midst of these pressures one's marriage and family are slowly shunted to a lesser order of priority. Work, church, community responsibilities, and other activities take precedence over time spent with one's spouse. Marriage takes time, effort, and commitment if it is to grow and develop. This needs to be emphasized in churches and elsewhere. Encourage people to make marriage a high priority item in terms of the expenditure of time and effort. Marriage enrichment seminars can help and so can discussion groups, the reading of helpful books, video tape programs that discuss marriage, and biblical sermons dealing with marriage. Try to stimulate couples to do things together and for each other. Help them establish priorities, work toward mutual goals, and think of ways to bring variety into their marriages. Married people are not the only members of the congregation who need help in learning how to communicate and deal with conflict. When there is gossip, backbiting, insensitivity, and stubbornness, there also will be tension and conflict.

By teaching Christians how to get along with one another, we help them build better relationships within the family and without. Married people, for example, should be shown the importance of listening, self-disclosure, mutual acceptance, and understanding. Empathy, warmth, and genuineness do not need to be limited to counseling sessions. These attributes can be learned and practiced in marriage and throughout the church, like individual couples who often are reluctant to seek counseling. For some this is embarrassing and maybe seen as an admission of failure. In contrast it can be emphasized from the pulpit and elsewhere that going for counseling can be a sign of strength. Often the counseling is most effective when it is bought early, not after the problems have grown progressively worse. Marriage is the most intimate of all human relationships. When this relationship is good and growing, it provides one of life's greatest satisfactions. When it is poor or even static and routine, it can be a source of great frustration and misery. God surely wants marriages to be good, a model of the beautiful relationship between Christ and his church.

The Christian counselor who understands biblical teaching and who knows counseling technique is best qualified to help couples attain the biblical ideal for marriage. In a good marriage, all things work together for the good, because we have learned, by the grace and love of God, to point them in that direction.

Conclusion

Finally, the revelation of God in Christ puts divine love into human history imbues it with human emotion and vulnerability, and it locates it with the weak outcast and despised. The notion of the fruits of the spirit, which reoccurs throughout Paul's epistles, illustrates that the love which is God is always seen in human acts of purity and caring.

Love, personal experience, and renewal of society are inseparably bound together. Grace becomes the restoration of the courage to love, in both personal and political life, based n the conviction that history is the locus of God's action. The philosopher Immanuel Kant was influential in promoting a view of Christian ethics that placed all the emphasis on reason to the exclusion of feeling. The Christian love commandment was to be explained as the Universalist principle of respect for all rational beings as ends in themselves and never as mere means. The spiritual dimensions are profoundly significant in helping couples become aware of their potential for being loving individuals in a marriage relationship. As the therapist is aware of and trusts the transcendent power of God, the source of love, the couple in marriage therapy will have increased possibilities of recognizing themselves as spiritual beings with the goal of reflecting that love within the marriage relationship.

The stated aim is to make good marriages better and implicitly, the goal is to foster personal growth and mutual fulfillment in enough marriages that the public image of marriage as a fulfilling relationship will be enhanced. When we are able to be honest with what we are feeling, and why we cannot forgive our partner, we actually are beginning the first step to healing our marriage, your partner has faults, and making peace and love with those first so you can solve the everyday conflict, will benefit everyone who relies on your marriage for their well-being.

Theologically, along with enticing persons to make their marriages more perfect by mastering skills of sharing feelings, the movement might also give greater acknowledgement to the ambiguity, the frailty and the incompleteness of human existence. The love and responsibilities demanded by such an enduring promise supply an opportunity for the full depth of relationship between husband and wife. However, the alarming divorce rate, the talk about temporary commitments and the lack of support in our culture for the preservation of marriage should make you pause and ponder. A marriage that lasts for life demands love and loyalty, along with God's grace and peace.

Biography

1—Comparing the marital satisfaction of clergy and lay couples, J. of Pastoral counseling, (1995).

2—Marriage ministry in midlife women, J. of Religion and health, (1982).

3—Marriage and Family enrichment, by H.A. OTTO, Ed.

4—L. Hof and W.R. Miller, Marriage Philosophy Process and Program, (1981).

5—Communication: Key to your Marriage, by H. Norman Wright, (Oct. 31, 2012).

6—People skills. How to assert yourself, listen to each other, and resolve conflicts by Robert Bolton, (Jun. 6, 1986).

7—The 10 Commandments of Marriage, by Ed Young and Beth Moore, (Aug. 1, 2004).

8—How to save your Marriage alone, by Ed Wheat, (Sept. 20, 1983).

9—Let's Get Rid of Social Security, by E.J. Myers.

10—Marriage: A Taste of Heaven Vol. 2, God's people make the best lovers, by Patsy Rae Dawson, (Sept. 1, 1996).

11—Boundaries in Marriage, by Henry Cloud and John Townsend, (Aug. 8, 2002).

12—How We Love: Discover your love style, enhance your marriage, by Milan Yerkovich, (Jan. 15, 2008).

13—Sacred Marriage: What if God Designed Marriage to make us Holy more than to make us Happy, by Gary Thomas (Jan. 29, 2002).

14—Christian Marriage, by Thomas Bear, (Dec. 6, 2011).

15—Spiritual Marriage, by Dyan Elliot, (Oct. 16, 1995).

16—Marriage on the Spiritual Path, by Shakti Parwhat Kaur Khalsa, (2007).

17—Created to be his Help Meat: Discover how God can make your Marriage Glorious, by Debi Pear, (Dec. 1, 2004).

18—Marriage Rules: A Manual for the Married and Couple up, by Harriet Ierner, (Dec. 13, 2012).

19—The Marriage Plot: A Novel, by Jeffrey Eugenides, (Sept. 4, 2012).

20—Passionate Marriage: Keeping Love and Intimacy Alive in Committed Relationships, by David Schnarch, (April 27, 2009).

www.ingramcontent.com/pod-product-compliance
Lightning Source LLC
Chambersburg PA
CBHW050402290526
45786CB00003B/1096